Bad Behaviour

Published on the occasion of Bad Behaviour,
an Arts Council Collection exhibition toured
by National Touring Exhibitions from
the Hayward Gallery, London, for Arts
Council England

Exhibition tour:

Longside Gallery, Yorkshire Sculpture Park	7 November 2003 – 11 January 2004
Aberystwyth Arts Centre	31 January – 20 March
Swansea, Glynn Vivian Art Gallery	15 May – 27 June
The Hatton Gallery, University of Newcastle	3 July – 15 August
Carlisle, Tullie House	15 January 2005 – 27 February

Exhibition curated by Emma Mahony
Selected by Isobel Johnstone and Emma Mahony

Catalogue and typography design by A2-GRAPHICS/SW/HK
Printed in England by Perivan White Dove

Published by Hayward Gallery Publishing
London SE1 8XX, UK
© Hayward Gallery 2003

ISBN 1 85332 235 0

Hayward Gallery Publishing titles are distributed outside North
and South America by Cornerhouse Publications, 70 Oxford Street,
Manchester M1 5NH, UK (Tel. 0161 200 1503; Fax. 0161 200 1504;
email: publications@cornerhouse.org; www.cornerhouse.org/publications).

For further information about works in the Arts Council Collection,
please write to Isobel Johnstone, Curator, Arts Council Collection,
Hayward Gallery, SBC, Royal Festival Hall, London SE1 8XX.

Bad Behaviour

from the Arts Council Collection

Arts Council Collection

Contents

Wetherilt and Jonathan Jones of Hayward Gallery Publishing.
Their combined adventurous and open approach and attention
to detail have resulted in an intriguing publication for which
they are due a hearty vote of thanks.

Lastly, but as ever by no means least, I thank all the artists
whose bad behaviour has inspired this show.

Susan Ferleger Brades
Director, Hayward Gallery

The Arts Council Collection is the largest national loan collection of post-war British art
in the world. It is continually touring in exhibitions organized by the Hayward Gallery and
by other galleries, and is on loan to public buildings throughout Britain. Changing displays
of sculpture in the Collection are regularly on view at Longside Gallery at Yorkshire Sculpture
Park, but otherwise the Collection does not have a permanent showing space. The Collection is
run by the Hayward Gallery on behalf of Arts Council England and is based at the Hayward
Gallery, South Bank Centre, in London, and at Longside Gallery at Yorkshire Sculpture Park.

For further information about the Arts Council Collection, please write to Isobel Johnstone,
Curator, Arts Council Collection, Hayward Gallery, Royal Festival Hall, London SE1 8XX
or email: ijohnstone@hayward.org.uk.

Bad Behaviour
Emma Mahony

Selected mainly from recent Arts Council Collection acquisitions,
Bad Behaviour charts a subversive streak in contemporary art and
focuses on a generation of artists who challenge convention and over-
turn established principles and social codes. Exploring instances of
anti-social and rebellious behaviour, the artists range from those who
subvert art historical frameworks to those who infiltrate and corrupt
the wider social and political realm. A group of artists whose works
attempt to undermine the purity of formalist abstraction direct their
attack towards art institutions. Others focus on the broader social
context, targeting national and political institutions with anti-
establishment sentiment. Yet others explore concepts of excess, self-
destructive behaviour and taboo. Although the works sometimes seem
disparate, an air of cynicism, a colloquial vocabulary and a scata-
logical humour links many of the works.

Anti-Establishment

Contemporary art has adopted many of the modes of expression used
by protest culture throughout the last few decades, from mobile props
such as placards and T-shirts to the rhetoric of political rallies. This
'language of protest' has been adapted by Martin Boyce, Ross Sinclair
and Bob and Roberta Smith to comment upon the futility of such strategies in the contemporary context. Although employing a didactic idiom,
these works no longer retain the political meaning of the sources from
which they borrow.
    Martin Boyce resurrects the political placard in his work
Souvenir Placards (Standard Edition), 1993 (cat. 10). Displayed on
the gallery floor, the placards are relics of a past generation. Boyce
has appropriated these emblems of protest culture and, by bringing
them into a gallery, has neutralized their once poignant messages.
Phrases such as 'Pay no poll tax', 'Make love not war', 'Free South
Africa' and 'Coal not Dole' invoke memories of past political causes,
all of which have long since been won or lost and bear little relevance
to today's society.
    The T-shirt slogan is the subject of Ross Sinclair's work. A popular
means of self-expression from the 1960s onwards, the T-shirt slogan
was often used to signal the wearer's nonconformity. Like Boyce's
Souvenir Placards, slogan T-shirts have lost their political vibrancy
and have been adopted by popular culture as a forum for rude jokes,
crass puns and clichés. Sinclair's series T-Shirt Paintings 1–80, 1993–
98 (cat. 38), all hand-painted with slogans, puns, song titles and phrases culled from literature, philosophy and popular culture, acknowledge

that the T-shirt is no longer a political tool, but an instrument of consumerism. They are memorabilia belonging to a past era: 'Bad Cop No Donut', 'Don't Do The Time If You Can't Do The Time', 'White Riot' and 'Jesus Is a Woman Too'.

Historically, protest is associated with the mobilized masses. When an individual takes it upon themselves to protest, they are often seen as a crank, as is the case when artists Bob and Roberta Smith adopt the role of the crazed political orator in the video Make Art Not War, 1997 (cat. 40). The rhetoric of protest is the inspiration for this work. Balanced precariously on a soap box, Bob Smith delivers a quasi-political speech in which he makes the case for art as a blueprint for a better future: 'The act of making art is society's way to find a new model for the future.' Despite his apparent attempts at earnestness, we are left unconvinced as to the validity of his cause. This is not surprising given the outrageous fabrications that form the basis of Bob and Roberta Smith's oeuvre, most notably their trademark text paintings. Although Janis Joplin... (Idiot Board), 1997 (cat. 39), refers to the cue cards made to help actors remember their lines. The work spins an amusing but highly misleading anecdote about the rock star Janis Joplin, who tragically overdosed on heroin in a motel room in Los Angeles at the age of twenty-seven, misattributing songs by the Beatles, the Rolling Stones and Frank Sinatra to her: 'Although Janis Joplin was compleetly [sic] deaf and really old she was still able to write two of her best song [sic] Strawberry Fields Forever (I Cant Get No) Satisfaction and My Way.'

Cynicism is key to the approach of a group of artists who direct anti-establishment sentiment at our national institutions. The monarchy, the Ministry of Defence and news agencies are the respective targets of Jonathan Parsons', Jason Coburn's and Henry Bond and Liam Gillick's scrutiny. Although politically subversive, their work is somewhat tongue-in-cheek.

Parson's jibe is directed at the national emblem of the United Kingdom, the Union Jack, which he has rendered in black and white. His choice of title asserts the work's art historical precedents: the title Achrome, meaning without colour, was used by the Italian artist Piero Manzoni in a famous series of paintings in the late 1950s. Parsons' Achrome (cat. 35), made in 1994, is an enlarged version of one of an earlier edition of five flags by the artist, also reduced to a representation of their tonal values.

Jason Coburn's Push the Button, 1996 (cat. 12), has been made on Ministry of Defence headed paper. The artist has never revealed how he came upon the paper and this question remains part of the myth surrounding the work. There is a conflicting play between the words scrawled in black ink onto the waterlogged paper in Push the Button – 'that's it', 'come on', 'do it', 'oh God' – and the civic importance of the letterhead onto which they are written. The title is a double entendre,

simultaneously a play on the button that could be used to activate nuclear warheads and on its sexual connotations. The subject relates to another series, the Noisy Neighbour Kit Project, where the artist faithfully transcribes the moans — heard through his walls — of his 'noisy neighbours' in the act of lovemaking.

Henry Bond and Liam Gillick's photograph 11th February 1992; Evacuation and closure of Whitehall and surrounding area due to discovery of suspected device. Trafalgar Square, 1992 (cat. 6), is one of a series of photographs taken by the artists at press events. In an attempt to examine the processes that underscore the dissemination of information, the artists assume the role of photo-journalists and show up at so-called 'news events' to make their own documentation of the events that unfold in front of them.

The work of Jeremy Deller and Gregory Green deals with the inherent powerlessness of the disenfranchised and explores how, in some cases, such individuals have resorted to civil unrest and terrorism due to an inability to effect political change through peaceful means.

Jeremy Deller's History of the World, 1998 (cat. 15), describes how culture has tracked the disintegration of no longer viable economic systems such as coal mining. Taking the form of a flow chart, the work traces a subjective musical lineage from Brass Bands to the Acid House music of the Manchester club scene. Both are arguably forms of folk music with a Northern tradition that can be linked to civil unrest: colliery Brass Band music embodied civic pride and the might of the industrial North, while Acid House reflected the inverse, the loss of that power and its consequences — disillusionment and alienation. The diagram includes socio-economic links, such as Pit Bands, De-industrialization, the Miners' Strike and Orgreave and more subjective associations including Melancholy, the North, 808 State, Techo and Detroit.

Terrorism, the subject of Gregory Green's work, is a product of powerlessness, where the insurgent forces resort to violence and surprise tactics to achieve their goals. Unlike Deller's armchair approach, Green assumes a pro-active role, becoming what he refers to as a 'conceptual terrorist'. Green's installation, Work Station No. 5 (London 1996), 1994 (cat. 22), resembles a crime scene from which the culprit has made a hasty retreat. The paraphernalia strewn across the work bench hints at some sinister activity. An open suitcase is packed with what looks like a ready-made bomb, while another lies half-made on the workbench, pending only the addition of one ingredient — Semtex. The location suggested in the title 'London 1996' would imply that it was once the hide-out of a dissident IRA terrorist plotting a campaign of terror. Green is notorious for his 'recipes', almost-complete bomb kits and convincingly simple constructions of missiles and other instruments of terror usually supplied with

instructions detailing how to manufacture them in the comfort of your own home – suggesting to us that anyone can play this dangerous game.

Anti-Formalism

The political establishment is not the only area critiqued by the works in this book, the art establishment is also fair game for the jibes and satirical gestures of the artists. The severe reductions of Minimalism and the purity of formal abstraction are aesthetics of twentieth-century practice which are subverted by the works of Adam Dade & Sonya Hanney, Gary Webb, Claire Barclay, Lucy Wood and Richard Wilson. Webb and Dade & Hanney corrupt the purity of formalist abstraction by introducing representational elements into their work while Barclay, Wood and Wilson subvert the form and function of familiar objects, often rendering them dangerous or useless.

Adam Dade & Sonya Hanney's film Stacked Hotel No. 6, 2000 (cat. 14), documents the systematic dismantling of the contents of a hotel bedroom, right down to the fixtures and fittings and their re-assembly in a neat pile. This subversive activity is conducted behind closed doors and drawn curtains and in hushed tones. The artists begin by making a video inventory of the furniture in situ, before they unpack a sinister assortment of tools and begin the job at hand. Their endeavour becomes incredibly labour-intensive as chairs, tables and neatly-folded bed linen are constantly rearranged. It slowly becomes apparent that the destruction of the hotel room is only secondary to their quest for the perfect sculptural assemblage of the room's contents. Once this has been achieved they film the 'stack' before reassembling and replacing all of the furniture exactly where they found it. The film is the only evidence that their performance took place. When viewed, the finished work has a modesty that belies its radical proposition.

Gary Webb's sculptures form curious unions of disparate elements, often combining found objects with industrially fabricated and hand-made components, and occasionally recorded sound or neon light. His often overloaded structures refer irreverently to the background of Modernist abstraction that inspired them. Where the Modernist trajectory is said to have been concerned with abstracting elemental forms from nature, Webb's sculptures are riddled with unresolved and uncon-nected representational elements. They embrace all that is inorganic, resulting in a kind of supermarket or Las Vegas aesthetic. As the artist has noted, 'I've definitely grown up with a relationship with huge indoor shopping malls, indoor drive-in areas, indoor everything.'[1]

Defamiliarizing familiar objects and subverting their function by rendering them dangerous or useless is also the territory explored by Claire Barclay and Lucy Wood. Many of Claire Barclay's works have associations with the domestic, but by making simple alterations to their physical appearance they take on more sinister associations.

The bristles that would have once covered the pole in Barclay's, <u>Untitled</u> <u>(pole with shaved-off bristles)</u>, 1994 (cat. 3), are shaved down to stumps, making the object look more like a weapon than a brush.

Lucy Wood's works have the potential to maim or even kill. <u>Can't Play, Won't Play</u>, 1996 (cat. 47), developed from an earlier project where Wood spent several years collecting condemned playground equipment from local councils. Climbing frames and roundabouts that had caused injury to their users were removed by the artist and exhibited alongside their casualty statistics. We are privy to their tragic histories but simultaneously distanced from them as these once dangerous objects of play are reinterpreted as museum pieces. <u>Can't Play, Won't Play</u> forms part of a body of work where Wood alters gym equipment, rendering it functionless and usually hazardous. Here she replaces the canvas of a trampoline with a sheet of plate glass — the consequences of using this trampoline could be fatal.

Displacing notions of the inside and outside, the public and private, and the familiar and unfamiliar, Richard Wilson's work challenges the structures that contain art. His works often take the form of temporary interventions where he literally cuts into or physically alters the fabric of the gallery. In some works, he introduces vast structures into the gallery, such as a domestic greenhouse which is cut into a partition wall adjacent to the ceiling in <u>High Rise</u>, 1989, and the garden chalet that is tipped upside down onto its pitched roof in <u>Lodger</u>, 1991. For <u>Facelift</u>, 1991 (cat. 46), Wilson takes another object of domestic leisure, the caravan, slices it in half and inserts a large trailer-like form into the resulting aperture. The trailer fills the shell of the caravan and extends outwards in a crude, windowless steel and wood extension. The title <u>Facelift</u> would suggest that the artist has made an improvement but his intervention into the structure of the caravan looks more like a strange growth or mutation.

Excess

Other works epitomize the term 'bad behaviour', testifying to instances of anti-social and self-destructive behaviour. Episodes of excess run throughout the works of Gilbert & George and Jim Lambie, while Oliver Payne & Nick Relph's films explore the intersections between youth and musical subcultures.

Gilbert & George's video work <u>Gordon's Makes us Drunk</u>, 1972 (cat. 18), is a performance piece in which the artists become intoxicated by Gordon's gin. Set in the front room of their house in East London's Fournier Street, the artists pour glass after glass of gin, sipping it in a slow and stately manner. A gramophone in the background pumps out Elgar and Grieg while a voiceover intones the words 'Gordon's makes us drunk'. As the artists become increasingly drunk the voiceover changes to 'Gordon's makes us very drunk' and 'Gordon's makes us very,

very drunk', and so on. Simultaneously a spoof and a celebration
of Britishness and high manners, Gordon's Makes us Drunk reveals
the point where habitual drinking becomes, as the artists put it,
'not a pleasure, but a duty to perform'.

Jim Lambie's Ultralow, 1998 (cat. 25), could be read as a contemporary response to Gilbert & George's earlier work. Named after a
brand of cigarettes with a supposed lower quantity of nicotine and tar,
Lambie is filmed smoking his way through an entire packet of Silk
Cut Ultralow cigarettes in the dark. The edited footage is superimposed
to reveal a pitch-black room illuminated only with tiny pinpoints
of flickering light from the glowing cigarette ends. Any likely health
benefit gained from smoking cigarettes with reduced tar is rendered
futile by his excessive consumption.

A figure who embodies this notion of excess is the subject of
another of Lambie's works: the legendary Sex Pistols bassist Sid Vicious.
Lambie's Sid Vicious, 2001 (cat. 26), features a commercially available
poster of Vicious smoking a joint. Together with a portrait of Kurt
Cobain, the work forms a series of portraits of two of rock's young
nihilists, both of whom committed suicide. The circumstances surrounding their deaths are not dissimilar — both had turbulent relationships
with their partners and both reached an impasse of sorts in their
careers. Several months after the Sex Pistols broke up, Sid Vicious
stabbed his lover Nancy Spungen to death with a hunting knife in
New York's Chelsea Hotel. Four months later he ended his own life,
distraught without her. At the age of twenty-seven Kurt Cobain, the
former lead singer of Nirvana, shot himself in the head in his home
in Seattle, believing he had nothing left to say to the world. Cased
in a Perspex box with four of the poster's corners folded in, partially
concealing the subject in their black glitter covering, Sid Vicious
can be read as a tribute to the dead anti-hero.

Oliver Payne & Nick Relph's Mixtape, 2002 (cat. 36), is a
twenty-three minute visual poem set to Terry Riley's 'Poppy Nogood
and the Phantom Band' from the 1969 album A Rainbow in Curved Air.
Structured tightly around the music, the footage is cut to the jarring
shifts and relentless rhythm of Riley's hypnotic soundtrack. Unlike
Payne & Relph's earlier films where 'found' footage is edited together,
the scenes in Mixtape are elaborately staged as dictated by Riley's
multi-layered score. A vague narrative cuts from tangentially related
vignettes (always in time with the score) — a Starbucks employee
covering her facial piercing with plasters; a skinhead with a diamond
encrusted pet tortoise on a lead; and a girl dancing in the corridor
of a block of flats — back and forth to the spasmodic writhing of
the young band members. The work examines the crossovers of youth
and musical subcultures, documentary filmmaking, nostalgia and
memory, while paying homage to Terry Riley's experimental and
ground-breaking music.

<u>Taboo</u>

Designed to provoke and offend, the works of Sarah Lucas and Grayson Perry assault social norms and conventions. There is an unsettling relationship between the taboo subject matter of their work and the medium in which it is expressed.

Sarah Lucas' representations of women and men use scatological humour and a colloquial vocabulary to challenge accepted notions of morality. Her <u>Self Portraits 1990–98</u> (cat. 29) depicts the artist in a series of confrontational and macho poses. She is frequently captured with her legs splayed apart or with a cigarette hanging from the corner of her mouth, glaring out at the viewer. Taken from a recent body of work where Lucas obsessively covered domestic items with Marlboro Light cigarettes, <u>Willy</u>, 2000 (cat. 30), is one of a series of three garden gnomes with phallic names: <u>Dicky</u>, <u>Nobby</u> and <u>Willy</u>. Aside from the obvious sexual connotations, these works hint at death and a gradual road to self-destruction.

Grayson Perry's works subvert conventions of art and craft and simultaneously launch an assault on British social mores and conventions. He has described himself as 'a self-confessed hater of contemporary ceramics who only keeps on using clay because pottery is held in low esteem in the art world.'[2] Despite their similarity to the forms of traditional vases, Perry's crude ceramics are built using coil and slab building techniques emphasizing his amateur status: he learnt ceramics at evening school. The pots are decorated with all manner of taboo subject matter, from scenes of deviant sex to satanic rituals and dismemberments.

For the most part, the artists in <u>Bad Behaviour</u> could be described as subtle subversives, making works that quietly infiltrate institutional structures. Often their means are playfully intrusive, lightened by a measure of cynicism and a tongue-in-cheek sense of humour. On occasion we are presented with the aftermath, the scene of a crime from which we are invited to deduce our own narrative. In other instances potentially dangerous objects and scenarios are sanitized by their relocation in the neutral confines of the gallery. But running through all of the work is an unspoken acknowledgement of the ultimate futility of their nonconformist strategies. It is not their mission to effect political or social change but merely to comment on and analyse pre-existing strategies, often only to point out how dated and inapproprioate they are in our contemporary climate.

Notes
1. Gary Webb, 'Interview with Iwona Blazwick', in <u>Early One Morning</u>, London, 2002, p. 155.
2. Grayson Perry, quoted in Louisa Buck, <u>Moving Target's 2, A User's Guide to British Art Now</u>, Tate, London, 2000, p. 131.

Plates

Martin Boyce

Ross Sinclair

Bob and Roberta Smith

Jonathan Parsons

35
Achrome, 1994
(installation shot)

Jason Coburn

MINISTRY OF DEFENCE
Main Building, Whitehall, London SW1A 2HB
Telephone (Direct Dialling) 071-21-8
(Switchboard) 071-21-89000

that's it

there

come on

do it

oh god

Henry Bond and Liam Gillick

11th February 1992; Evacuation
and closure of Whitehall and
surrounding area due to discovery
of suspected device. Trafalgar
Square, 1992

Jeremy Deller

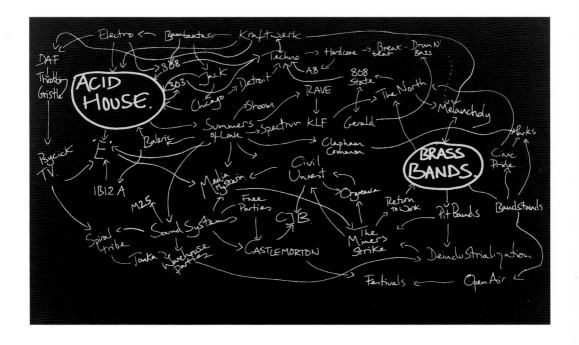

Gregory Green

21
Pipe Bomb #3 (LA), 1993
22
Work Station No.5 (London 1996), 1994
(installation shot)

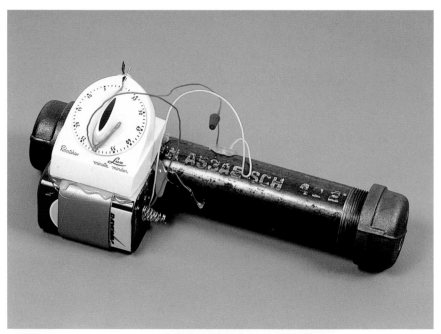

Adam Dade & Sonya Hanney

Stacked Hotel No. 6, 2000
(still)

Gary Webb

44
Clap, 1997
(installation shot)
45
Mirage of Loose Change, 2001
(installation shot)

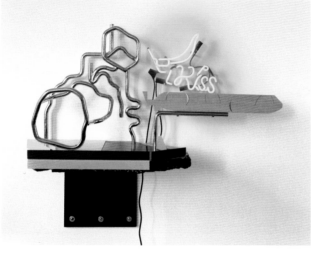

Claire Barclay

3

Untitled (pole with shaved-off
bristles), 1994
(installation shot)

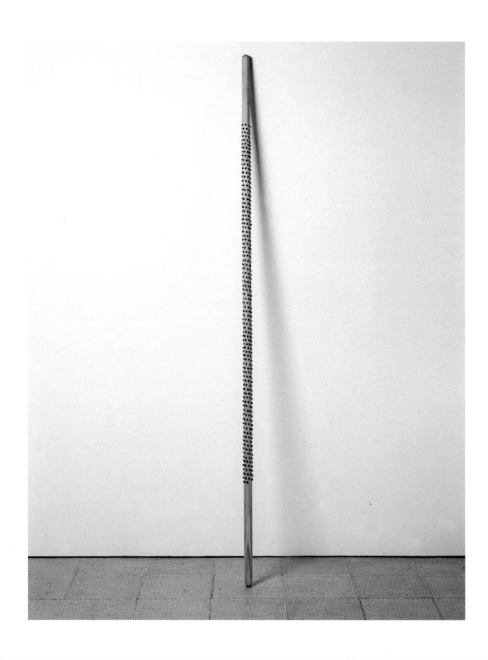

Lucy Wood

Can't Play, Won't Play, 1996
(installation shot)

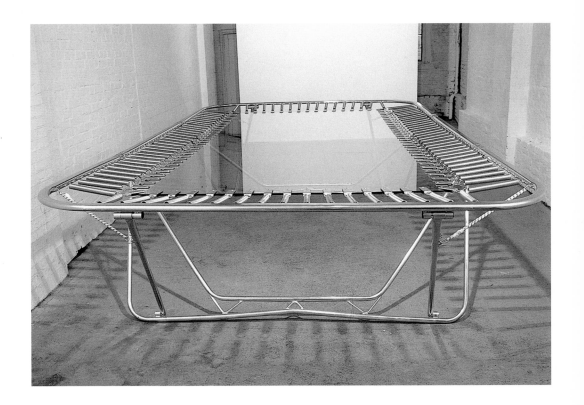

John Isaacs

Jordan Baseman

4
Based on Actual Events, 1995
5
Moist Secret, 1995

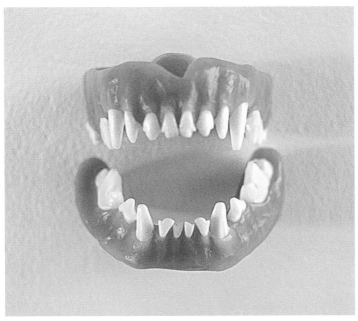

Adam Chodzko

2101 Km/Hr (Secretor), 1993
(installation shot)

Martin Creed

Richard Wilson

Gilbert & George

"GORDON'S MAKES US DRUNK"

Summer 1972

Sculpture on Video Tape

NO. 6 OF 25

george and gilbert

the sculptors

'ART FOR ALL' 12 Fournier Street London E1
01-247 0161

Jim Lambie

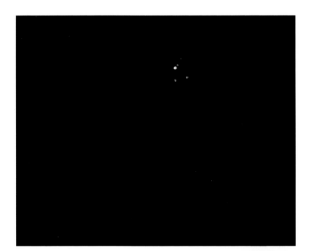

Oliver Payne & Nick Relph

Sarah Lucas

29
Self Portraits 1990—98

From left to right, top to bottom:

Self Portrait with Fried Eggs, 1996
Fighting Fire with Fire, 1996
Got a Salmon On #1, 1997
Self Portrait with Mug of Tea, 1993
Divine, 1991

Self Portrait with Knickers, 1994
Self Portrait with Skull, 1997
Human Toilet II, 1996
Smoking, 1998
Eating a Banana, 1990
Summer, 1998

Human Toilet Revisited, 1998

Grayson Perry

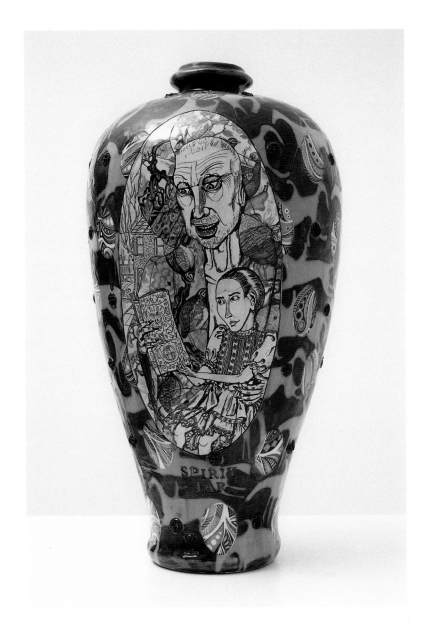

Small-Scale Works and Multiples

1
Fiona Banner
Inside-Out Aviator Glasses, 1994

7
Terence Bond
Untitled (Brick), 1989

2
Claire Barclay
Anodyne, 1994

8
Terence Bond
Untitled, 1995

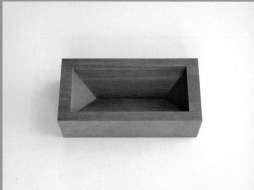

27
Michael Landy
We Leave the Scum with
No Place to Hide, 1995

28
Colin Lowe and
Roddy Thomson
Swallow Seed Menu, 2003

19
Dan Graham
One, 1992

20
Andrew Grassie
Pleiadian Space Craft, 2000

24
Tania Kovats
Virgin in a Condom, 1990

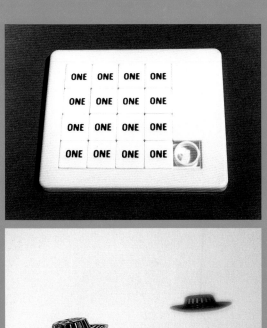

77/

31
Jeff Luke
Dowel and Wire, 1994

33
Lucia Nogueira
One and Three, 1994 (detail)

32
Adam McEwen
I Want to Live, 1993

34
Cornelia Parker
Meteorite Lands on..., 1998

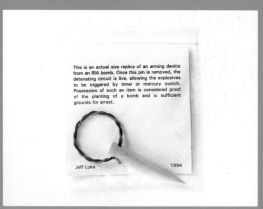

This is an actual size replica of an arming device
from an IRA bomb. Once this pin is removed, the
detonating circuit is live, allowing the explosives
to be triggered by timer or mercury switch.
Possession of such an item is considered proof
of the planting of a bomb and is sufficient
grounds for arrest.

Jeff Luke   1994

41
Jessica Voorsanger
David Cassidy's Diet, 1994

43
Mark Wallinger
A Real Work of Art, 1994

42
Jessica Voorsanger
Susan Dey's Beauty Tips, 1994

9
Christine Borland
Carrier, 1994

16
Jeremy Deller
Karl Marx 18.12.2000, 2000

17
Anya Gallaccio
Couverture, 1994

List of Works

Dimensions are in centimetres, height x width x depth. Page references are to illustrations in this book. Some works will not be shown at all venues.

1 (p. 75)
Fiona Banner
Inside-Out Aviator Glasses, 1994
aluminium, mirrored glass
6.5 x 14.5 x 14.5
edition no. 3 of 50
purchased from Sarah Staton, 1994

2 (p. 75)
Claire Barclay
Anodyne, 1994
cotton fabric, leather and feathers
pillows: 10.8 x 38.6 x 29.1,
strap: 13.2 x 31 x 32.7
unlimited edition
purchased from the artist, 1994

3 (p. 47)
Claire Barclay
Untitled (pole with shaved-off
bristles), 1994
wood (pine) and mixed fibre bristles
224 long, 3.5 diameter
purchased from the artist, 1997

4 (p. 53)
Jordan Baseman
Based on Actual Events, 1995
dogs' teeth, dental acrylic
6 x 7 x 9
gift of Charles Saatchi, 2002

5 (p. 53)
Jordan Baseman
Moist Secret, 1995
wax and oil
6 x 6 x 3
gift of Charles Saatchi, 2002

6 (p. 37)
Henry Bond and Liam Gillick
11th February 1992; Evacuation and
closure of Whitehall and surrounding
area due to discovery of suspected
device. Trafalgar Square, 1992
r-type photograph and text
photograph: 49 x 67, text: 30 x 21
purchased from the artists, 1993

7 (p. 75)
Terence Bond
Untitled (Brick), 1989
brick, dyed wood veneer
on plywood and paint
12 x 21.5 x 10.7
gift of Charles Saatchi, 2002

8 (p. 75)
Terence Bond
Untitled, 1995
coconut fibre and ink
46 x 76 x 4
gift of Charles Saatchi, 2002

9 (p. 76)
Christine Borland
Carrier, 1994
de-activated gun, polythene
51 x 21 x 3.2
unlimited edition
purchased from the artist, 1994

10 (p. 27)
Martin Boyce
Souvenir Placards (Standard Edition), 1993
wood, emulsion and gloss paint
7 placards, dimensions variable
gift of Charles Saatchi, 1999

11 (p. 55)
Adam Chodzko
2101 Km/Hr (Secretor), 9468 Km/Hr
(Secretor) and 9605 Km/Hr (Secretor), 1993
manifestation juice (food dye and
glycerine), lead crystal, plastic,
acrylic and acetate
3 works: 36.5 x 12.3 x 5.3, 29.5 x 10.5 x 5.7
and 34 x 12 x 3
gift of Charles Saatchi, 1999

12 (p. 35)
Jason Coburn
Push the Button, 1996
ink on paper
29.8 x 21
purchased from Lotta Hammer, 1997

13 (p. 57)
Martin Creed
Work No. 135, 1996
aluminium, cement, plaster and emulsion
50.8 x 50.8 x 25.4
purchased from the artist, 1996

14 (p. 43)
Adam Dade & Sonya Hanney
Stacked Hotel No. 6, 2000
VHS video with sound
running time: 235 minutes
edition no. 1 of 5
purchased from the artists, 2001

15 (p. 39)
Jeremy Deller
History of the World, 1998
screenprint
66 x 112
edition no. 37 of 100
purchased from Paul E. Stopler, 1998

16 (p. 76)
Jeremy Deller
Karl Marx 18.12.2000, 2000
portfolio containing colour photographs,
text, envelope and card
portfolio: 74 x 48.3 x 3.3,
5 prints each 30.5 x 40.6
edition no. 1 of 5
purchased from Cabinet Gallery, 2001

17 (p. 76)
Anya Gallaccio
Couverture, 1994
chocolate, coconut butter, aluminium
and printed paper
20 x 17 x 17
purchased from Karsten Schubert, 1994

18 (p. 61)
Gilbert & George
Gordon's Makes us Drunk, 1972
videotape and framed certificate
running time: 9 minutes
purchased from Nigel Greenwood Inc, 1973

19 (p. 77)
Dan Graham
One, 1992
plastic,
7.5 x 9.2 x 0.8
unnumbered edition of 500
purchased from Yves Geraert, 1994

20 (p. 77)
Andrew Grassie
Pleiadian Space Craft, 2000
metal
6 diameter
purchased from Mobile Home, 2000

21 (p. 41)
Gregory Green
Pipe Bomb #3 (LA), 1993
metal, plastic, glue, wire and paint
34.3 x 10.2 x 14.6
gift of Charles Saatchi, 2002

22 (p. 41)
Gregory Green
Work Station No. 5 (London 1996), 1994
mixed media
dimensions variable
gift of Charles Saatchi, 2002

23 (p. 51)
John Isaacs
Say it isn't so, 1994
mixed media
204 x 129 x 132
gift of Charles Saatchi, 2002

24 (p. 77)
Tania Kovats
Virgin in a Condom, 1990
resin, rubber, paint and wood
11 x 3 x 3
edition no. 4 of 12
purchased from Laure Genillard
Gallery, 1994

25 (p. 63)
Jim Lambie
Ultralow, 1998
Betacam sp
running time: 15 minutes
edition no. 2 of 10
purchased from The Modern
Institute, 2000

26 (p. 63)
Jim Lambie
Sid Vicious, 2001
printed poster on foamboard with
black glitter
43 x 60 x 20
purchased from Sadie Coles HQ, 2001

27 (p. 80)
Michael Landy
We Leave the Scum with No Place
to Hide, 1995
aluminium, ink, wood and Perspex
94 x 19 x 19
edition no. 1 of 6
purchased from Ridinghouse
Editions, 1995

28 (p. 80)
Colin Lowe and Roddy Thomson
Swallow Seed Menu, 2003
mixed media
42.7 x 50 x 6
edition of 10 and 2 artists' proofs
purchased from Sadie Coles HQ, 2003

29 (pp. 68–69)
Sarah Lucas
Self Portraits 1990–98
iris prints; 12 works; edition no. 24 of 50
purchased from Sadie Coles HQ, 2000
© Sarah Lucas 2003. Courtesy Sadie Coles
HQ London

Titles, dates and dimensions as follows:
Eating a Banana, 1990, 78 x 82
Divine, 1991, 78.8 x 90.8
Self Portrait with Mug of Tea, 1993,
92.7 x 75
Self Portrait with Knickers, 1994, 98 x 73.1
Fighting Fire with Fire, 1996, 97 x 73.3
Human Toilet II, 1996, 97.7 x 71.4
Self Portrait with Fried Eggs, 1996,
98.2 x 73.3
Got a Salmon On #1, 1997, 98 x 72.5
Self Portrait with Skull, 1997, 97.3 x 70.8
Human Toilet Revisited, 1998, 81.5 x 77.3
Smoking, 1998, 97.3 x 71.6
Summer, 1998, 84.5 x 77.2

30 (p. 67)
Sarah Lucas
Willy, 2000
plastic, tobacco, paper and glue
86 x 42 x 34
purchased from Sadie Coles HQ, 2002
© Sarah Lucas 2003. Courtesy Sadie Coles
HQ London

31 (p. 78)
Jeff Luke
Dowel and Wire, 1994
wood, wire, paper and grip-seal bag
5 x 10.4 x 0.9, bag 13 x 11
unlimited edition
purchased from Imprint, 1993
© Jeff Luke Estate 2003. Courtesy
Jeff Luke Estate

32 (p. 78)
Adam McEwen
I Want to Live, 1993
suede and cotton
23.9 x 10
unlimited edition
purchased from Sarah Staton, 1994

33 (p. 78)
Lucia Nogueira
One and Three, 1994
glass, mercury, phosphorus, paint,
platinum, velvet and cardboard
2 ear-rings, each 5.2 x 1 x 1.8
edition no. 1 of 13
purchased from the artist, 1994

34 (p. 78)
Cornelia Parker
Meteorite Lands on…, 1998
printed and burned paper
5 works, each 54 x 69
edition of 20
purchased from the Multiple Store, 1999
A Multiple Store Commission

35 (p. 33)
Jonathan Parsons
Achrome, 1994
polyester, cotton, wood and rope
457 x 228
gift of Charles Saatchi, 1999

36 (p. 65)
Oliver Payne & Nick Relph
Mixtape, 2002
DVD with sound
running time: 23 minutes
edition no. 11 of 20
purchased from Gavin Brown's
Enterprise, 2002

37 (p. 71)
Grayson Perry
Spirit Jar, 1994
earthenware
45.7 x 20.3 x 20.3
purchased from Laurent Delaye
Gallery, 2002

38 (p. 29)
Ross Sinclair
T-Shirt Paintings 1–80, 1993–98
gesso and acrylic on cotton
80 parts, each approximately 61 x 61
purchased from the artist, 1999

39 (p. 31)
Bob and Roberta Smith
Although Janis Joplin… (Idiot Board), 1997
signwriters' paint on board
4 parts, total 243.8 x 487.7
purchased from the artist, 1998

40 (p. 31)
Bob and Roberta Smith
Make Art Not War, 1997
VHS video with sound
running time: 11 minutes
edition no. 1 of 5
purchased from the artist, 1998

41 (p. 79)
Jessica Voorsanger
David Cassidy's Diet, 1994
rice, rubber, tetracycline and polythene
3.2 x 19.4 x 20.9
edition of 50
purchased from Sarah Staton's Superstore,
Laure Genillard Gallery, 1994

42 (p. 79)
Jessica Voorsanger
Susan Dey's Beauty Tips, 1994
biscuits, toothpaste, Ex-Lax and polythene
3.2 x 20.9 x 17.5
edition of 50
purchased from Sarah Staton's Superstore,
Laure Genillard Gallery, 1994

43 (p. 79)
Mark Wallinger
A Real Work of Art, 1994
wood, brass, polyurethane,
plastic and paint
12 x 12.8 x 7.3
unnumbered edition of 50
purchased from Anthony Reynolds
Gallery, 1994

44 (p. 45)
Gary Webb
Clap, 1997
plastic, aluminium, microphone
and electrical components
25 x 36 x 10
gift of Charles Saatchi, 2002

45 (p. 45)
Gary Webb
Mirage of Loose Change, 2001
chrome, steel, plastic, granite,
wood and neon light
108 x 132 x 47
purchased from The Approach, 2001

46 (p. 59)
Richard Wilson
Facelift, 1991
wood, steel, aluminium and cloth
274 x 269 x 188
gift of Charles Saatchi, 2002

47 (p. 49)
Lucy Wood
Can't Play, Won't Play, 1996
glass and steel
150 x 289.6 x 502.9
gift of Charles Saatchi, 1999